Speak with Chic

One woman. Ten truths.

Angel Charmaine

Jessica,

I pray my story inspires you
to give voice to your own!!

Love & Light,

Angel Charmaine
11/2/2018

I dedicate this book to my sons,
Tyler, Kevon, Kajel and Asher.
I stood up in the face of fear that tried
to tell me I shouldn't, couldn't, wouldn't,
and boys, mom did it!
You can do anything your mind can conceive.

To my Sistahcousin, Sapphire Starr, thank you for
keeping Alice at bay while I was finding myself.

"For God hath not given us the spirit of fear, but of
power, and of love, and a sound mind."
2 Timothy 1:7 (KJV)

CONTENTS

INTRODUCTION

The more time you spend being afraid to do something
the less time you have to do anything. – Angel Charmaine

I had to write this book. I had to write it because I was afraid to write it. Afraid of sharing. Afraid of not doing it right. Afraid of being ridiculed. Afraid of failure. Afraid of success. I knew if I did not face this fear, I would remain stagnate. Without knowing the *how*, I decided to focus on the *what* and *just start writing.*

This book is the first in the *Speak with Chic – One woman. Ten Truths* Series. Each book contains ten conversations that chronicle my life, decisions, choices, mistakes, accomplishments, failures, and successes. Sharing these conversations, helps me heal and grow, and I pray others will read my stories and find a way to courageously, confidently, and boldly speak up and give voice to their own truth in their own unique way.

FALL IN LOVE IN THE SHOWER

I fell in love with a woman at forty years old, and I met her in the shower. Actually, I have known her since she was a baby. We were childhood friends. This beautiful, energetic, talkative, smiling little girl was my best friend in the whole, wide world, and when we were kids, the whole, wide world was a ginormous place filled with people, possibilities and places. As little girls, still wearing pigtails playing hopscotch and learning to write cursive, we did what my brothers called "girly things" like have tea parties and play with doll babies. It was always the two of us. Even as we got older, and I realized there were other girls I could play with, talk to, have at our tea parties; she was still my favorite of them all.

As we got older, other people entered my life who were not as kind, friendly, or as happy as my best friend and I were together. Some people didn't like my best friend and began to say things about her I had never heard. At first, I did not believe them, but the more people talked and the more they showed me *evidence* of the things they said, I began to believe them. Before I realized it, we were not best friends anymore. We weren't friends at all. By the time we were fifteen years old, I had totally walked away from my best friend.

I saw her in passing throughout the years. We would stop, and chit chat every now and then. Each time we ran into each other, she seemed to be so happy and full of life. She seemed to never age as if she had been unscathed by life. She would always say, "Girl, life doesn't bother me. I know everything will be okay, and it's all good." I was always amazed by her strength, and she never brought up the fact that I was the one who ended our friendship. Of course, I always felt guilty during the meet ups because even though she did not bring it up, I knew what I had done. Years later, I noticed something about those random run-ins; she never left before me. In fact, I never actually saw her leave at all because I was always the one either too busy or too ashamed to stay.

Twenty-five years later, we met again, but this time was different. I met a group of women, and we talked every day about everything. I allowed myself to be vulnerable and shared my life and thoughts with them as they shared with me. It got to a point where I began to talk about my dreams and aspirations. Suddenly, and I do mean suddenly, I started to do what I was talking about. I envisioned, created, incorporated and started a business within two weeks. While working the new business, I bumped into my best friend, and this time, I was the excited one. I talked and talked and talked. She just listened and stood with this silly – no, not silly but adorable – smile on her face. I stopped talking and just looked at that smile. Then, I began to smile. I stood in the shower and smiled, and for the first time in many years, I embraced my best friend and sobbed and attempted to explain to her why I walked away. I tried to tell her all the things I had heard, and I tried to explain how I wanted to make amends, but the abuse, the neglect, the mistakes, the pain was all I had to share when we would meet, and how all she ever had to share was joy. She didn't say a word; she just listened.

When I was all cried out, I spoke aloud while standing in my shower with the hottest water my skin could bare and water washing away now quiet tears, and I said to myself, "I understand, and I forgive you. I love you, and I have never stopped being your best friend."

SHOWER REVELATIONS

The shower is my sacred place. I go there to hear myself think and to understand things more clearly. Life's stuff - inside, outside and around – doesn't seem so overwhelming while I am in the shower. I reason with myself and ponder life's secrets there.

I believe it is the water. The soft yet forceful way it rains on my skin from the shower head. Maybe it's the way the water washes away the dirt and grime of the day from my body. I watch the dirt trickle down the drain taking with it the cares of my day or the restlessness of my night.

It could be the heat. Let me tell you, every time I step into a shower and the water caresses my skin, I thank God for hot water especially on a cold, winter morning. Hot water awakens me and invigorates me. It hugs me and reassures me that the night is over, and it is a new day. My mind becomes creative, innovative and uninhibited. The idea to write a book came to me while in the shower.

Let me tell you. I had a little talk with myself.
Me: Are you going to write a book about these conversations we have in this shower."
Myself: Yep.
Me: What? For real?
Myself: Yep, I am going to write a book, and you know what?

Me: What?

Myself: I am going to be a published author.

Okay, you get the idea of how that conversation went down, but after the "whats" and "for reals," I thanked God for the vision and thanked Him for the manifestation.

Shower revelations are ideas, epiphanies, life lessons that help to cleanse my soul, reconnect with my spirit, and create positive change in my life. The idea to write and share these thoughts stemmed from a biblical verse, Revelation 12:11 (NLT), "And they have defeated him by the blood of the Lamb and by their testimony." Immediately, I thought, YES! I must share my testimony with others. For me, writing has been therapeutic. Many shower revelations became journal topics. I journal to find answers, to find sanity, to find solutions, to make sense out of seemingly senseless things. These revelations have been life lines to keep me sane and in the game.

Your place of serenity may not be the shower. It may be the garden, the bedroom, or the car. Whatever the place, go there when you need to quiet the noise of the world to hear yourself think, to feel and to be restored. When you do this, the right thoughts will come to your mind and revolutionize your life.

FULL GROWN

I grew up. I don't quite remember when that happened. It just did. I liked all frilly things - doll babies and tea parties. And really that's about all I remember. Oh, and my 7th birthday party, or should I say my seven years old birthday party because I believe it's the only one I ever had. I shared that day and that party with my brother who turned eight years old five days after I turned seven. We had a half princess half G.I. Joe cake. That's all I remember.

Now, I am forty years old, and I am all grown up, but I absolutely cannot recall when that happened. Childhood scurried past me just as responsibility raced towards me, and everything is now a blur. What was real? What was made-up? I can't tell the difference most days. I cannot remember names of friends I acquired because we moved so often. At some point, my brain simply flipped off the "remember names" switch, and let me tell you, that dang switch has been broken ever since. Even now, on any given day, I can't remember which of my children's names fits which child. I just yell out all four, and the one I want comes running. I think they have created some system to decipher the code of the Four-name yell – TylerKevonKajelAsher. It never fails, the right one shows up every time.

As a kid, we moved from this State to that State; from this neighborhood to that neighborhood; from this school to that school; from this relative's house to that relative's house. I attended eight different schools between two different cities before I reached high school, and we weren't in the military. High school is where I found some semblance of stability and normalcy. I got accustomed to moving and going until I ran straight through high school with very few memories and even fewer special moments.

At forty, I am still moving and going. I've upgraded from bouncing amongst neighborhoods, cities, schools, states and added jobs and countries to the list.

At some point on my life's journey, I realized and acknowledged that I had learned to be a runner. Yes, I even became a runner for exercise, but that's not what I'm referring to here. I learned to run from things that hurt, things I didn't understand, things I didn't like. Believe it or not, I even learned to run from things that I really wanted – talk about self-sabotaging behavior. To make things worse, while running away from stuff, I was simultaneously running toward stuff. I learned to set goals and strive to attain them. Sounds good, right? But ask yourself this question. How can a person run in two different directions at the same time, be sane, and most of all get anywhere? Exactly, I don't know either. Although, I was cognizant and acknowledged this dynamic, I did not know how to change it, and in the meantime, I felt like I was caught in a trap and losing time.

The past few years leading up to my 40th birthday, I had been asking myself, "how do I stop running, and how do I get free from the trap?" What an important and life altering question, right? Well, maybe not that profound for you, but for me, the answer changed everything. The answer came my way during a shower revelation. These little nuggets of wisdom I believe God drops directly into my spirit which typically happens while I'm in the shower. Go figure. Anyway, the answer was very simple – stop running…stop chasing…be still and be present. Sounds easy enough, right? In my brain, I was discombobulated. If I am being still, how am I going to get anything done, and what do you expect me to do while I sit and do nothing, and exactly how do you "be present?"

The answers to these questions did not come during that shower revelation. Oh no, that would be too easy - too much like right. I still don't have all the answers. However, I have learned that being still and being present are learned behaviors just like running and chasing, and it's a daily process to hone them. It takes a level of courage and fortitude to stay still when everything in you is screaming, "ruuuuun." It takes patience and faith to sit and wait on promises to be fulfilled without being given a time line. It takes a massive amount of trust to believe everything has a purpose, a time and a place; trust that what is for me is really for me, and ultimately trust myself. I had to believe that if I am still, I will not be destroyed. I will not die. I will be okay, and I will thrive.

To make memories, I must be still and embrace the present. I must purposefully smell the coffee brewing and listen to the sounds of the water splashing; listen to my children laughing and telling silly jokes; allow myself to stop and laugh aloud because that silly joke was quite funny.

To pay attention and relish the intricate moments of my life is to be present. To be present and embrace those moments is to truly live. To live without fear of not falling backwards or not reaching the top but to just *be* is freedom.

JUST ONE OF THEM DAYS

Somedays, I get a fullness in the center of my chest – dab smack in the middle of my breast. There's something stuck in my windpipe; it's not a tangible thing like food or water, but it cuts off my ability to effectively talk and communicate. Something presses down against my shoulders; it's not strong enough to render me bedridden but heavy enough to ensure my efforts are unproductive. My pulse is racing, but I'm standing still. Hundreds of insightful, useful, elaborate words prance around in my head, but I lack the stamina it takes to exercise the facial muscles needed to allow my mouth to formulate such hefty words, therefore, effortless, monosyllabic, emptiness trickles out as I attempt to communicate with my children.

My children. My babies. My boys. There are four of them. Four teenage boys, well, one of them is what some folks call a tween, but this year, he will be a teenager too. I love my handsome, mighty men of valor. My boys are rather amazing and not just because they are mine. Ask anyone who's spent any time with them, and they will tell you the same. They are funny as all get-out. All are athletic, artistic and academically astute. The eldest is a senior in high school; the twins are freshman, and my baby boy is in the 7th grade. Teachers adore them, church people love them, random folks praise them, yet their mother is utterly overwhelmed trying to rear them.

A typical day in the life of Char – the single mom. The alarm clock on the phone sings at 5:30am. On good days, I get a 30 – 45 minutes workout and cook hot breakfast for my boys before they leave for school by 7:25am. Yes, I'm a working mom, so I'm off to work shortly after they are out of the door and headed to school. After a day of paid work ends, mommy Uber is on duty for free. I drive to pick-up children from school to take home for snack and to change clothes. I drive from home to sport practice and back home to cook dinner. By the time dinner is cooked, it's time to pick-up from practice and return home for showers, homework, dinner, discussion, play, arguments, fights, tv, games, clean-up and bedtime.

These are not seamless activities. There is often some crying and yelling spread throughout the evening events, and we try diligently to have it all done by 10:30pm. Who needs more than 7 hours of sleep – give or take an hour. When the day is done, and night begins, the real work happens - the behind the scenes stuff. I sit at the computer to pay the bills. I sift through the trailer load of papers sent home from teachers for my signature and my money. I rob and beat-up Peter to pay Paul to ensure my children can participate in the activities that will give them

an opportunity to live to their fullest potential and be great.
Finally, I dig deeply into the middle of some unseen place
and extricate the necessary thing, whatever the thing is at
the time – hope, love, strength, courage, energy, sanity –
that will help me have just enough peace to fall asleep and
do it all over again tomorrow.

Every now and then, *that* day happens. You know
the day. The day the fullness in your chest seems
unbearable and you feel like throwing the baby away with
the bathwater, the tub, the potty, hell, the whole damn
bathroom. Each child is exerting his temperament in his
own way. Each child has an issue with another child in the
house. None of the children seem to be able to do anything
they're supposed to do; all are being rebellious, and
everyone hates me – mom.

If you are expecting me to give a five-step process
on how not to be overwhelmed by your kids, don't wait for
it. I have no clue. I have a Master's Degree in Counseling
and Psychology. I have taught other people's children for
15+ years, but I have yet to figure out how to not lose my
shit with my own kids. I have no profound insight to share.
What I *can* tell you is I have accepted that sometimes there
will be days like this. Days when I want to get in my
vehicle and just drive – no specific destination -
somewhere, anywhere away from the chaos that is my life.

I can tell you some days I am going to feel full and heavy and unproductive. Some days, I am going to yell at my kids and send them to bed with peanut butter and jelly sandwiches for dinner. There will be days when I sit in front of the television, watch romantic movies on Netflix that make me feel good about life and love, drink wine and eat popcorn. I can also tell you that these days don't last forever and having one every now and then is not going to kill my kids and does not make me a bad mom. That last part, the part about not making me a bad mom, is the most difficult concept to embrace.

After four years of undergrad, two years of graduate school and a couple years under my belt as a teacher, I was confident that I was competent in my profession. Sure, I had different students every year and worked within different schools and systems, but with a little adjustment and professional development here and there and the help of other educators, I believe I was a good teacher. On the contrary, after 17 years of motherhood and four children, reading books and articles, and listening to sundry advice of other parents, I still feel I was doing this thang wrong. However, on "lose your shit days," I sit myself down and say, "Self, they are alive and healthy. They are excellent students. They are great friends. They are talented athletes and musicians. They are kind and considerate. They are good humans." Then, I say, "Self, they didn't get that way alone. You play a major part in shaping them. You are doing something right." After that little pep talk with myself, I resolve to just let it go. Let go of the fear of failure as a mom. Let go of my thoughts of what I think other people think of my parenting skills, and I embrace the fact that I am going to get overwhelmed from time to time, but I have the power to change the course of any day at any time as soon as I choose to take dominion over my thoughts and speak words of power and life. Then, I commence to marathon watch Netflix movies, eat popcorn and drink wine until tomorrow comes, and I get back to the business of doing my best to give the world the best me possible along with four other good humans.

2 A.M. Cry

I'm lying here in my bed at like 2 o'clock in the morning – in tears. I don't really know why or how my childhood molestation became an issue tonight. I look at my phone, it's literally 2:16a.m., and I am writing. I feel the need to write this off my chest, write this off my mind.

Tonight, I find myself wondering if I should tell the man for whom I'm falling so deeply about my little incident. I know to call it a "little" incident implies it wasn't that serious, but so often I don't believe it was that bad. I mean, I hear the horrible stories other women tell, and quite frankly, I should feel lucky that my own situation was not like theirs. Right? I mean, I don't have breakdowns around men, and I can be in intimate relationships.

Actually, I have been in too many intimate relationships; I often wonder if that is a symptom of the incident. Sometimes, I don't even know if I remember the entire thing correctly. At times, I have flashback memories, but I have been able to live and thrive without this creating limitation. I don't want to be treated like a victim. At the same time, I'm smart enough to know that I didn't walk away totally unscathed. I just don't know what to attribute to *it,* or if I should attribute anything to *it*. I feel to attribute any behaviors to the incident, current or past, is to scapegoat, and I don't ever want anyone to think I am trying to find an excuse for my own bad decisions or any mistakes I've made. At the same time, I know all our experiences shape us in some way, so why should I put more emphasis on this experience than any other.

The incident does not define me, and at the same time, I feel like I want people closest to me to know, so they can understand why I'm ultra-protective of my kids; why the thought of my 17-year-old son staying out with friends at night without me scares me shitless; why I need the man I fall in love with to reassure me at every turn that he really does believe I'm beautiful, wonderful, intelligent, and sexy - and mean it – for real – to reassure me that there is no other motive behind what he is saying to me.

I want people I love the most to know and not know – all at the same time – that I know they think I'm one of the strongest women they know, but deep down inside, I feel tainted, small, weak, unsure, unbeautiful, dumb, unlovable. However, to say any of this to anyone other than this page is to somehow become the victim – which I am not. Therefore, every now and then, I have a 2a.m. cry. It usually comes out of nowhere for no apparent reason. It's a silent cry. One where my face is all wet, and I can't really see the words I'm writing because of the waterfalls. A cry so silent my back and chest ache because of the effort it takes to not release a sound.

My children would never understand why mommy is making such a gut-wrenching sound, and I surely will not traumatize them, so this 2a.m. cry must remain silent. The tears do subside, and eventually, there will be one lone tear that rolls from my eye, to my nose, down my lip, and somehow, it just evaporates. I'll stop writing, drift to sleep and this 2 a.m. cry will have never happened.

MASK OFF

December 10, 2017, marks five months on my loc journey. I created a YouTube channel to chronicle the journey. I know, I know. You didn't know that. I know you didn't know because there are only about ten views of my videos – 10 views total. Anyway, I post at least once a month to see the growth and change in my hair. Little did I know this hair journey would teach lessons aligned with my life journey.

Prior to November, I had been diligent about making the videos. I felt good about the way my hair was growing and how it was beginning to take on a look of its own which is different from the twists from which they began. When November 10th rolled around, I was excited about my four months of progress and even more excited because I learned something new. I learned how to rinse my hair with apple cider vinegar (ACV) and decided to do a video of me rinsing my hair with the ACV mixture. I made the video, but it never made it to YouTube. As I reviewed the video, all I could focus on was my face. I didn't see how shiny my hair was or how much the ACV concoction had removed the buildup and product residue from my hair and dumped it all into the water in the sink. All I could see were imperfections and scars.

My doctor says I have a condition called Polycystic Ovary Syndrome (PCOS). I had never heard of the term before he said it. In a nutshell, PCOS is a condition where my hormones are imbalanced and causes some not so great and not so traditionally pretty things to happen inside and outside my body. One of those not so pretty things is the growth of facial hair. Yup. That one. Most people don't even notice, but it is difficult for me to see anything else, and on the fourth month of my loc journey, the video I intended to chronicle the growth of hair on my head instead chronicled the growth of hair on my face – up close and personal. Let me break here and say, it was a good video. My hair looked fabulous. The proof that an ACV rinse really works was evident in the once clear now murky water, but I did not post the video. The idea of thousands of people looking closely at the scarred skin on my face caused by years of facial hair growth was unbearable. Yes, I know only about ten people watch the videos, but in my mind, this would be *the* video thousands of people would choose to watch – the one with my scarred, stubbly face. Nope, the video could not be posted.

It's the fifth month of my loc journey, and I realize not only did I not post that video, but I did not create another video to chronicle the fourth month. An entire month of my process is absent, and now, there is a void, a small one, but one none the less. I ask myself, "Self, that was a good video, so why didn't you post it?" I don't know about you, but when I start talking to myself and asking questions of myself, things get deep. If you really want to get to the nitty gritty, don't call your best friend just talk to yourself. I find it extremely difficult to lie to myself or give myself excuses that I believe. The answer to the question is no secret to me, but one I usually glance over and pretend doesn't exist.

The answer is simple, yet the reality is difficult for a *seemingly* strong, self-loving, confident woman like myself to acknowledge. For me, to acknowledge a thing makes it real, and if that real thing is a problem, I now must deal with it and figure out how to resolve it. I'm just built like that. If you tell me you have a problem, my brain automatically begins looking for solutions. I look in the mirror and answer the question, "Up close and personal, I am not pretty enough to post the video. These scars are ugly; people are going to laugh and mock me."

Lawd, I wasn't ready. A question about a hair video unlocked and opened a door that led me to thoughts I did not realize I have about myself. The initial reaction is to shut that damn door and carry-on. Then, a quote from a book I recently read entitled *Detours* by Tony Evans, rushed to my mind. "Growth can only occur in a spirit of honesty." Yep. Ouch. Now, I know I have got to deal with some stuff. It's funny how we never seem to get rid of all our stuff. As soon as you spring clean your life, it's winter. You look for protection against the elements and realize you can't find anything because of all the summer and fall stuff you've collected. I am beginning to think we never fully get rid of all our stuff. We just learn to live and thrive between periodic cleanings.

I created my company, Speak with Chic, LLC, in October 2017. It's a movement all about embracing truth and giving voice to your own truth and experiences. I had to have another conversation with myself. Yes, I have them often. I ask, "How can you expect to help others embrace and speak their truths if you are still covering up your own?"

I know somewhere early in my life, I embraced some ideas. Ideas I have told myself and have accepted for most of my life. I don't believe they came from any one individual but from a myriad of experiences, conversations, situations. Some of the ideas are things like I am kinda cute but not beautiful. I can talk but not too loudly and not about…that. I make good grades, but I'm not that smart. I can set goals but not too lofty. I should be thankful when good things happen to me but don't *expect* them to happen. I can have some success but only this much. All lies.

It's funny how a video about hair helped me to acknowledge and address the lies I have silently whispered to myself. Lies that have no doubt hindered growth in every aspect of my life.

I, now, choose to stop self-sabotaging and believing the lies. I choose to embrace love, light and life. I am fearfully and wonderfully made. I am beautiful. I am intelligent. I have enormous goals that I will attain, and I do expect and accept greatness into my life. I choose to take off the mask and to be honest with myself and others, so I can experience real growth and see the fruit of my labor. Like Tony Evans said, "growth can only occur in a spirit of honesty." No more lies.

PAIN + PASSION = PURPOSE

Something hit me about 10 years ago. My Jesus friends might call it a revelation. My teacher friends might call it an epiphany, and my tribe (oh, I'll talk about them later because that's a whole 'nuther' story all by itself) might say I got woke. Either way, this revelational (that probably ain't a word) epiphany that got me woke happened during a time when I could not seem to grasp an understanding of much of anything.

It was a time when I had a heap of questions and absolutely no answers. Simple little questions like: How does a good God allow a bad man to hurt an innocent little girl? What made me marry a man I did not love just because he was a *good* man? Why do I keep working a job that makes me physically ill? How the hell did I end up a twenty-something year old mama of four babies and not know what in the Sam Hill to do with them?

I was ready to throw all that glass is half full stuff in the trash with the rest of the half empty containers of spoiled milk. While driving my truck down Deans Bridge Road in Augusta, Ga, feeling extremely sorry for myself, emotionally numb, just plain old depressed with a face drowning in tears, something rose up in me, and I heard a tiny voice say, "No, that was not the plan for you. Because everything is connected and you all make choices that affect each other, sometimes I have to alter the plan to work things out for your good." Okay, I know somebody will not believe I heard this, but I did. The voice continued, "Remember the ugly, former things. Look and see that none of them stole your joy, destroyed your spirit, or killed your soul."

Now, here comes the revelational (still not sure that's a word) epiphany that got me woke. None of the pain and hurt of my past had taken me out. I was still in the fight. Overtime, I had become strong and sturdy, yet my heart remained warm and gentle. In fact, I became strong enough to sit here today and put my business in the street to help another woman have her revelational (uh, I'm pretty sure by now it's a word) epiphany that awakens her, so she can begin to speak her truth.

I haven't the foggiest idea of the right way to write a book. I'm not quite sure if I started correctly. I'm not quite sure if it should be this short or that long. My life is so busy being "mommy Uber" I haven't really had time to learn much about maneuvering this here computer. If it's any consolation, I attempted to research this thing prior to starting. I got such a hodgepodge of information from the slew of internet help articles I have been perusing until I think I'm even more confused than before I began the research. However, the one common bit of advice that resonated in me is to just start writing. So, that is what I did.

I learned a long time ago that writing is therapeutic. I cannot heal and continue to grow without sharing my experiences with others. Who knows, you may be on your very own Deans Bridge Road having a hard time navigating confusion and doubt, and the words in a little book covered in butterflies just might rise up and speak truth at the moment you desperately need a revelational epiphany awakening.

THE TRIBE

Everyone needs a tribe. Merriam-Webster defines tribe as "a social division in a traditional society consisting of families or communities linked by social, economic, religious, or blood ties, with a common culture and dialect." When I talk about my tribe, I am not referring to the traditional, technical meaning of the word. My tribe consists of women I have had the opportunity to connect with on my journey to learning about myself and living my purpose. Women from diverse generations, backgrounds, ethnicities, cities, states, countries, life experiences and temperaments.

God has divinely placed these women along the path at critical intersections in my journey, and they have and continue to encourage me, support me, love me, root for me, caution me, pray for me, share with me, laugh with me, get enraged with me and even cry with me, and I do the same for them without any judgement. They are my tribe.

Prior to finding my tribe, I had acquaintances and friends. Acquaintances are individuals I know and may hang out with from time to time, but the relationships don't have much depth and usually once the arena/situation changes in which I meet them, the relationship usually ends. Friends begin as acquaintances; however, situations/circumstances happen that create depth and require both parties to open-up, share and become genuine with one another.

Since my family constantly relocated, I never seemed to have enough time for acquaintances to become friends. However, in high school, I met one girl who befriended me. She then introduced me to her friend, and the three of us eventually became best friends. We were like the three musketeers. These are the girls with whom I sat and talked about boys. These girls know all my teenage secrets. They know the guy to whom I lost my virginity. Although, they probably can't remember his name; that was a mighty long time ago. Just in case you're wondering, yes, I remember his name. His name was Anthony. Now, if you ask for a last name, you would be asking too much.

I digress. Back to what I was saying. These girls know me, and I know them. They love me, and I love them. They are my oldest and dearest friends, and there are only two of them, and we are still friends. For years, I had my two best friends and a host of acquaintances. For a long time, I did not *do* new friends.

It is amazing how life begins to just *happen*. I had dreams and aspirations. I set goals and made plans, and I set off to college, and life showed up. My senior year in college during my last semester I got pregnant. Life decided to sit down and stay. I got a job. I got married. I got pregnant. I went back to college. I got pregnant. I got a job. I got overwhelmed. I got depressed. I got lost. I got sick, and I got tired. I got divorced. Life just kept on *happening*.

While life had shown up and was showing out, I realized it was quite the busy body, and life was spending time with my best friends too. I felt I had to deal with life all by myself. It's funny how the world is filled with so many people dealing with very similar issues, cares and concerns, yet we tell ourselves no one can help us, and we must just figure out life on our own.

I'm grateful God and divine plans are not swayed by my foolishness. Women began to enter my space. Women with whom I did not have cultivated, deep relationships but who still understood my situation, my pain, my confusion, my doubt, my anger, my hopes.

There was a time when I was so overwhelmed with the many roles I played - wife, mom, teacher, church lady, coach, mentor, daughter, friend, etc. - until I was on the verge of literally losing my mind. A woman who was also a mother of four children talked to me on the phone and somehow heard my distress even though my tone was calm, and she hurried over to my house, sat with me and talked me out of a dark place. At the time, I didn't realize I was depressed. When you're in the valley, sometimes, you don't know you're there until someone comes along to help pull you out. She could hear my pain and was willing to share her peace when I couldn't find peace for myself. She is a member of my tribe.

Throughout the past 13 years, these types of women have shown up and have helped usher me into the next leg of my journey. The affect each one has had on my life and the bonds created is often stronger than even that of a blood sister. These women spoke life and truth from their own experiences into my soul to help me get to where I am today. These women are members of my tribe, and the tribe is not a set, select, stagnate group. As I grow and my journey ebbs and flows, so does the tribe. Some have come and gone, and some came and refuse to leave. Time and space does not matter. I can connect with any of them at any time and be recharged, reinvigorated, reassured. They are my tribe.

BODY, SOUL and SPIRIT

I have done quite a bit of traveling; however, I was born and raised in Savannah, GA, and the place I call home is Augusta, GA. My mama is in Augusta. I met my oldest, dearest friends in Augusta. I fell in love with a man for the first time and fell out of love with myself all in Augusta, GA. I guess you can say I have a bit of a love/hate relationship with home.

One, sweet place I found in Augusta is a church home. The pastor is a tall, dark-brown skinned man with a kind smile and a respectable, admirable yet formidable disposition. He is from some little town in Alabama. You know he is good-n-country as soon as he begins to preach. He tears up the English language something awful; he even adds some new words. I would catch myself silently correcting his speech from my chair in the congregation. Despite learning new vocabulary words on Sunday mornings, I always understood everything he said, and when in his presence, I know I'm standing near a man after God's own heart. I learned a lot from Pastor's teachings while sitting in those pews.

One morning years later, across the country, in a different state, while taking a shower, I remembered something he spoke during a Sunday sermon.

We are a three-part being. We are a spirit, we live in a body and we possess a soul. Wow! Although I heard this many years prior, I have even repeated it to others throughout the years, on this day, I made a personal connection with the statement.

Sometimes, it is difficult to make a personal connection with a new idea when you don't have a traumatic or profound enough event with which to link it. I had just made amends with myself. I had just had an experience where I became fully aware that somehow and at some point, I had a schism within myself. Pastor's words at that moment made total sense.

Through the terrible things I have endured, my spirit endured. My spirit remained joyful. My spirit remained constant. My spirit developed and grew stronger through each test. My soul was battered, abused, frustrated, sad and angry. For twenty-five years, my spirit and my soul were not in concert, and my body was an outward manifestation of the discord going on within it. My weight was not consistent. Fat this year, not so fat next year. Really fat this year, not really that fat next year. Although I read, studied and listened to the Word, my feelings would not line up with the knowledge I was gaining, and my body as well as my life suffered from the disconnect. Anyone close enough and paying attention probably noticed my Dr.

Jekyll and Mr. Hide or better yet Mary and Martha life style.

Realize you are not a one-dimensional being. Take time to listen to each part – spirit, soul, body. Don't esteem one part over another. Understand they are equally integral parts of the whole – You. Nourish each part in its own way, and when you do that, they will work in concert to ensure you fulfill your purpose and live your best life.

WALK IN LIGHT

On New Year Day 2018, I got up and was lounging around doing much of nothing. About a week prior, I started watching motivational videos on YouTube. I ended up watching an old *Oprah Show* rerun about the video and book entitled *The Secret*. I heard about this book, but I always said to myself, "Ain't nobody got time to be thinking 'bout no Secret. I'm 'round here tryna live real life." Yep, that was me - stinking thinking. For years, I was opposed to *motivational* speaking. I heard in church that all that motivational talk is not what is going to get your spirit right with God. All that positive thinking stuff is just man-made mumbo jumbo and what I really needed to focus on was the Bible. If I would just read, study and meditate on the Bible, I could get right with God, learn how to stop all my sinning and back sliding and get on with the business of winning souls for Christ.

I figured my problem was just that I wasn't reading the Bible enough, so I read more. I think I ended up reading the Bible - not simply reading scriptures from the Bible but reading cover to cover like a novel - about three times. That may not seem like a lot, but if you factor in the all the chaos that was going on in my life as well as all the falling asleep I did while trying to read, you would understand three times cover to cover is a significant number of times for me to have read the Bible. After all that reading, I was still full of "can't get right."

On January 1, 2018, I watched about 35 minutes of the *Oprah Show* rerun. Rhonda Byrne, the author of the book, Lisa Nichols – I absolutely love this woman – Dr. Michael Beckwith, and a couple other people who teach the secret were on the show. Dr. Beckwith made a statement that sparked a shower revelation. He said, "Most people say the Presence or God's Presence is in everything, but the truth is everything is in the Presence." Ohhh my goodness! That statement reverberated somewhere deep in my core, and the more I thought about it the more excited I got.

I closed my eyes in the shower while the hot water pelted my skin, and I tried to envision packing God's presence inside my body, stuffing His infiniteness, His everythingness inside my body, and it just wouldn't fit. It would not fit. Then, I changed it around, and in my mind's eye, I began to see me inside His presence. I visualized myself inside this huge expanse of darkness. I said to myself, "turn the darkness to light." When you close your eyes, everything looks dark behind the eyelids, but if you are intent enough, you can change the darkness to light. It happens slowly, but you can see flashes of light behind your eyes until you see nothing but light. I stayed in that shower until all I saw was light. The expanse became light. I became part of the light.

God's presence is not in me, but I am always in His presence. He is everything, everywhere. He is I am that I am. Whatever it is that I want, need, desire, He is that. Here's the ah-ha - I AM ALWAYS IN IT. I do not need to try and add to me. I can stop trying to find it. I am in it. I got ridiculously excited about this. I closed my eyes and see myself in a massive expanse of light.

I remember the scripture, Psalm 23:4. *Yea, though I walk through the valley of the shadow of death, I will fear no evil: for thou art with me; thy rod and thy staff they comfort me.* You and I are not walking in darkness. Even at the lowest place in life, even at the point of facing death, we walk through the *shadow* of death. For there to be a shadow, light must be present. You don't get a shadow unless there is light. Light is always there. You are always in it. I am always in it. We are always in it. We are always living inside the presence of light and love – God.

ABOUT THE AUTHOR

Angel Charmaine, the mother of four, fabulous humans, has learned her purpose in life, has a vision, and has finally decided to speak her truth. She has a B.S in Education and a M.Ed. in Counseling and Psychology. She taught high school in Georgia, Tennessee and Kentucky with Department of Defense Education Activity (DODEA) schools, and abroad with Specialist Schools Academies Trust (SSAT) as an Education Consultant in Abu Dhabi, UAE. She is currently an Army Wounded Warriors Advocate.

Angel empowers women through her inspirational speaking, writing and entrepreneurship. Her vision is to help women learn to acknowledge, own, embrace, and give voice to their truth. Through Speak with Chic, LLC, she is working to create inclusive communities where women can connect with a tribe to encourage and inspire each other to be courageous, confident and bold.

Follow on social media.
Website – www.SpeakwithChic.net
Facebook – www.facebook.com/AuthorAngelCharmaine
Instagram - @Angel.Charmaine
Twitter - @speakwithchic

Real Women Real Reactions

I feel the raw emotion like a Mary J. Blige song. It has the essence and spirit of Maya Angelou's <u>I Know Why the Caged Bird Sings</u>. I LOVE IT. – Sapphire S.

I feel this story! I can feel every word. The energy resonates, and while there are notes of sadness, there is so much hope for the future– Unique B.

I didn't expect to feel the raw emotion and relate so quickly. -Whitney J.

This was an amazing read! -Lolita L.